CONSOLIDATION

LOCALITIES AFTER THEIR CAPTURE.

1.—CONSOLIDATION OF A CAPTURED SYSTEM OF TRENCHES.

The capture of a system of hostile trenches is an easy matter compared with the difficulty of retaining it. A thorough knowledge of the principles, a careful study and correct use of the natural features of the ground, and a detailed preparation and organisation of the work, are necessary; but success will only result if there is also an absolute determination on the part of all ranks to get the work done promptly at all costs.

The principles of the consolidation of captured trenches are, briefly, as follows:—

(a) To establish a series of strong points or centres of resistance, wired all round and mutually supporting each other according to the ground. These points should be provided with machine or Lewis guns at once.

(b) To provide good communication to the rear from these points.

(c) To fill in all hostile trenches within bombing distance of the points occupied.

(d) To establish, if possible, simultaneously with the consolidation of strong points in the front line, a number of supporting points in rear. These points should, if the ground is favourable, be placed to cover the intervals between the works in the front line.

(e) The strong points can later be connected to form a continuous front line.

The above principles must be applied with due regard to the natural tactical features of the ground. The satisfactory siting and consolidation of a position will largely depend on the power possessed by the Officers on the spot to recognise during the various stages of a battle the minor features of real tactical importance. This ability is only acquired by previous training, and is a quality which every Officer must study to possess. The size and trace of the "strong points," as well as the intervals between them, will vary according to the lie of the ground and the plan of the hostile trenches captured. During the process of consolidation concealment from artillery observation is of importance.

(B 12338) Wt. w. 3762—7584 120M 8/16 H & S. P. 16/381

The first essential is speed in rendering the captured position strong enough to resist the first counter-attacks. It is therefore necessary that a definite plan should be decided on beforehand as to which points first require attention. This can be done, in the majority of cases, with great accuracy from maps and aeroplane photographs and from a study of the ground from any point in our lines which commands a view of it. In the case of craters the forecast of the tunnelling officers must be obtained.

Although it is usually advisable that assaulting troops should be relieved as soon as possible, this must not be taken to imply that the duty of securing ground gained is the task only of the relieving troops. It is an unsound principle for troops to *expect* to be relieved immediately after an attack, as it wastes valuable time at a critical period when speed in work is essential. It must be understood that troops which take a position must commence the work of consolidation at once.

The distribution of R.E. detachments requires to be carefully considered beforehand. In all cases of an assault or advance, where it is intended to secure the ground gained, the troops destined for the purpose should include a detachment of R.E., the Commander of which should be detailed previously and attached to the staff of the unit or formation concerned.

Garrisons must hold on to their ground; they have nothing to fear from being outflanked.

2.—CONSOLIDATION OF LOCALITIES.

During an advance, when it becomes necessary to consolidate some locality of tactical importance, such as a village or wood, the same general principles hold good as in the consolidation of a system of trenches. Some notes on the particular points that require attention in the case of villages and woods are appended.

Villages.—Enlargements from even small scale maps give very accurate plans of most villages and make it possible to plan the defence in sufficient detail beforehand. It is essential that subordinate commanders should be provided with such plans, in order that the general idea of the defence may be quickly and properly understood.

The principles of the defence of a village are laid down in Infantry Training, Section 146. The order of urgency of work is as follows:—

(a) Barricade and picquet all exits. Establish centre of resistance near exits to cover approaches or any streams or tracks which might serve to guide a counter-attack. Commence work on keep, preferably at village crossroads. Barricade roads.

(b) Reconnoitre for cellars.

(c) Establish communications, giving cover from view, radiating from keep to outer centres of resistance, and from keep to the rear.

(d) Construct bombproofs in cellars at centres of resistance and keep—false roofs to cellars, etc.
(e) Complete keep.
(f) Improve communications at (c) above, to give cover from fire.
(g) Make lateral lines of communication between centres of resistance.

Centres of resistance should be established (if it is possible to do so) to the flank of conspicuous buildings likely to afford good targets for hostile artillery fire. In the case of keeps in villages, this is often impossible owing to the presence of church spires. It is, however, preferable to have a keep, even with this disadvantage, that is central, accessible and strong against infantry assault. It should be remembered in this connection that by the time hostile infantry can assault a village keep, hostile artillery fire will necessarily have ceased.

Woods.—As in the case of villages, plans should be prepared of the locality.

There has been much discussion in the past as to what part of a wood should be occupied. Experience has proved that, owing to the great advantages afforded by cover from view, the position to take up in a wood is, just so far within the outer edge as will permit of good view into the open. In this connection it should be remembered that in course of time shell and rifle fire thins out the edges of woods considerably. It is therefore advantageous in the first instance to take up positions slightly in rear of those which may appear at the moment to be most advantageous.

If, as is often the case, the wood is surrounded by a hedge, there is a natural tendency to make trenches against this hedge. This is to be avoided. A hedge forms a very good obstacle against assault, with the addition of a little wire. If it screens the view it can be quickly thinned.

The order or urgency of work is as follows:—

(a) Establish centres of resistance for all round defence at the corners and salients of the wood. These are the points which are most liable to counter-attack.
Establish central reserve, reconnoitre, blaze and clear communications.
The defence of a wood should be very active, and counter-attacks must be launched against any hostile troops that may reach the edge of the wood, in order to prevent a lodgment that places the enemy on equal terms.

(b) Establish intermediate centres of resistance and lateral communication.

(c) Establish central keep at junction of rides, or on near edge of clearing.

In the case of large woods and forests, where the general line of defence runs through a wood, a line of strong centres of resistance should be established across the wood, if possible behind a road or other clearing. The near edge of the clearing should be entangled, and the intervals between the "centres" should be swept by fire. As time permits "rays" should be cleared, radiating from the centres of resistance and crossing similar "rays" from adjoining centres, so as to add to the depth of the field of fire.

These rays should be wired and obstacles arranged, so as to break up an attack and force the attackers into the openings.

A line of intermediate centres, communications, &c., should also be established, as indicated in (b) above.

3.—OCCUPATION OF CRATERS.

i. The occupation and consolidation of mine craters presents many difficulties, and all ranks should understand the principles to be acted upon in the event of the explosion of mines on their front.

ii. Craters are usually formed as a result of one of the following mining operations:—
- (a) An attack by us on the enemy's trenches;
- (b) An attack by the enemy on our trenches;
- (c) Underground fighting.

iii. The possession of a crater offers the following advantages:—
- (a) It can be turned into a strong point capable of holding a small garrison;
- (b) It gives command of the ground in the vicinity;
- (c) It forms a considerable obstacle.

iv. (a) When mines are exploded by us in connection with an attack on the enemy's trenches, our object should be to seize and hold the whole of the mine crater or craters, or a line in front of them. The latter plan is usually the best, and the craters in rear can then be turned into strong points.

(b) When craters are formed as the result of an attack by the enemy on our trenches, or in the course of underground fighting, our object will usually be to seize and hold the near "lip" of the crater.

Parties must be rushed out at once to seize the lip. It may be impossible to open up communication to these parties till after dark. They should, therefore, take sufficient grenades, water, &c., and must be prepared to hold on though isolated.

v. Before the explosion of a mine a forecast should be made of the state of affairs to be expected after the explosion, and all details of probable requirements should be worked out. These would include:—
- (a) The formation of dumps of engineer materials as close up as possible.
- (b) The organization of working and carrying parties.

Work should start immediately after the explosion of the mine, and no time should be lost in turning into account the quiet interval which usually follows the explosion.

The personnel of R.E. Field Companies should be freely used for this work under instructions given through the General Staff.

vi. The following are the main points to be attended to in the actual consolidation of the craters :—

- (*a*) All trenches should be strutted as they are constructed. Special frames for this purpose must be made beforehand.
- (*b*) All works on a crater, whether inside or outside the "lip," should be provided with a parados.
- (*c*) Dug-outs should be made by tunnelling into the sides and not at the bottom of a crater.
- (*d*) At least two communication trenches should be constructed leading into each crater.

    Entrances to craters should be made at the sides and not through the rear "lip."
- (*e*) All trenches leading up to a crater from the enemy's line should be straightened or filled in for a distance of at least 40 yards from the position of the defenders, so as to keep the enemy bombers at a distance.

    This work can usually be carried out with the least difficulty immediately after the explosion.
- (*f*) Collapsible knife-rests, French wire and other forms of portable wire entanglement, should be brought up in large quantities and thrown over the " lip " of a crater.

vii. There are two main methods of holding craters :—

(a) *Method "A."* (*See* sketch on p. 6 and Plate A.)

This method should usually be employed after the explosion by us of a mine in the enemy's trenches or in the area where it is known that the enemy is not engaged in mining.

The front "lip" of the crater is held by means of several posts. Two communication trenches lead into the crater, one on each side, and give lateral communication between the posts. One or two dug-outs are constructed in the sides of the crater.

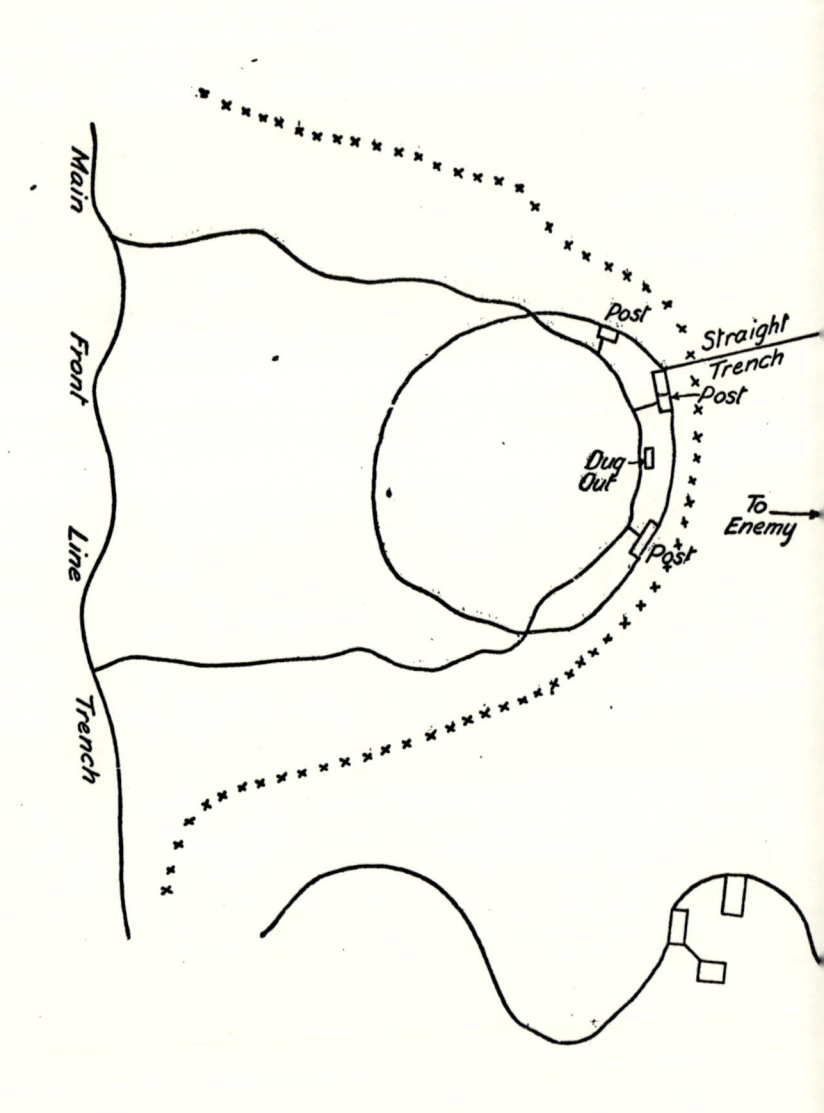

(b) *Method " B."* (*See* sketch below and Plate B.)

This method should usually be employed when the enemy has exploded a mine in or near our trenches, or when we have exploded a defensive mine close to our own trenches.

The rear "lip" of the crater is held. Wire is thrown inside the crater. One or two loop-holes are cut through the rear "lip" so as to command the inside of the crater.

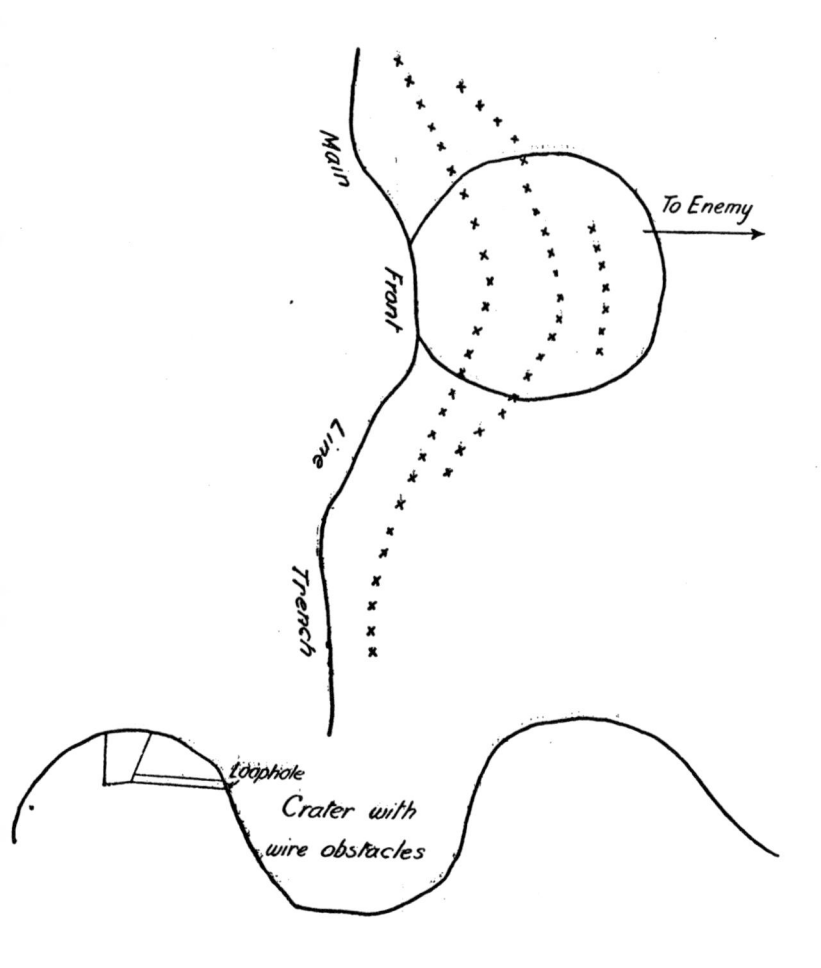

Plate C shows a scheme for converting the area behind the lips of a series of craters, which have been occupied, into a strong post.

The importance of rendering the means of access to the lip secure from bombing attack is not always recognized.

(viii.) Work should be carried out in the following order :—
- (*a*) Construction of one or two posts in the "lip" of the crater;
- (*b*) Wiring the front of posts and filling in or straightening trenches leading from it towards the enemy;
- (*c*) Digging of communication trenches up to the crater.

And, if far lip has been occupied :—
- (*d*) Digging trench for lateral communication inside the crater;
- (*e*) Completion of wiring front of crater and construction of further posts in far "lip";
- (*f*) Construction of dug-outs;
- (*g*) Improvements to the above.

It should usually be possible to do (*a*), (*b*) and (*c*) together.

4.—NOTES ON RAPID WIRE ENTANGLEMENTS.

One of the first requirements in consolidating a position is to get some wire out in front of it.

The following general principles regarding the construction of wire entanglements should be observed :—

- (i.) The rear edge of the entanglement should be about 20 yards from the trench; if the trace of the entanglement is irregular and does not follow the trace of the trench, it will make the task of the hostile artillery more difficult.
- (ii.) The depth of the entanglement should be as great as possible, and at least 30 feet. The wire available should be expended in forming a deep entanglement rather than a "heavy" one (*i.e.*, one with a large amount of wire between each set of posts). The construction of two belts with an interval between them, rather than one belt of twice the depth, gives the hostile artillery a deeper target to destroy, without increasing the material required for constructing the entanglement, except by one row of pickets.
- (iii.) There will seldom be time in rapid wiring to "dig in" the wire for concealment. Every advantage should be taken, however, of natural folds in the ground, long grass, or brushwood, or other means of concealment.
- (iv.) Wire entanglements should be 2 feet 6 inches to 3 feet high.

(v.) The posts in a row should be about 6 feet from each other, and the rows about 6 feet apart. If wooden posts are used they must be strong; light posts are useless.

(vi.) The difficulties of crossing an entanglement are increased if it is not too regular, e.g., if the heights of the posts above ground and the distances between them are varied. For rapid wiring drill, however, a regular entanglement is easier to construct.

To ensure that an obstacle can be erected with rapidity and in silence, every one of the working party must know what he has to do and work so that he does not get in the way of the others.

This necessitates some form of *drill*. There are a large number in use, of which a selection is given on pages 14 to 20.* The following notes and rules will be found useful in carrying out any form of drill for constructing wire entanglements :—

(i.) The party should, as far as possible, work so that the obstacle is always between them and the enemy. Each wiring party should have a double sentry lying down about 30 or 40 yards towards the enemy to prevent patrols sniping or bombing the party. If circumstances necessitate it, a special covering party should be provided.

(ii.) The party should work extended and not bunched together.

(iii.) Large parties, in which each group of men has only one operation or duty to perform, will erect entanglements quicker than a small party, in which each man has several duties to perform in succession, unless latter is very well drilled.

(iv.) The best *unit* of entanglement is about 40 or 50 yards long. Its construction can then be controlled from one point. This distance is also a convenient interval to leave small gaps for patrols.

(v.) A line of posts is best laid out at night by putting down a tape or string with the intervals of the posts marked by bits of rag or sandbag tied on to it.

(vi.) The end of a coil of barbed wire will be found secured on the drum tucked under the standing part. In the dark it is very hard to find and release. Coils should, therefore, be prepared by daylight. A good method is to attach a piece of string to the end, uncoil the roll half a turn, re-coil it on a piece of old sandbag and fasten it up by the string. The end of the wire can then be readily found in the dark. The pieces of tin on the wooden drums should be removed to prevent noise.

---

* A French method will be found in Appendix B "Notes for Infantry Officers on Trench Warfare."

It may be found convenient, to make carrying easier, to re-coil the barbed wire in smaller coils on a stout stake.

(vii.) Pickets should be made up into bundles of one man loads. They should be firmly tied with plain wire or brought up in sandbags. The latter is the surer way of keeping them together, at any rate with small wooden pickets. A drum of barbed wire is best carried over the shoulder, with a stout stake passed through it, which also serves for uncoiling the wire. Pickets and wire should be dumped by the carrying party, outside the trench, behind the centre of the length to be wired.

(viii.) Mauls, if used, should be muffled by nailing on a leather face or with sandbags. About 8 thicknesses of sandbag material are necessary to be of any use.

(ix.) Equipment should not, unless necessary, be worn by wiring parties, as it is liable to cause noise.

(x.) **Stays and holdfasts** (*see* Fig. 1).

Forward stays are not absolutely necessary if the entanglement posts are well driven in. They are usually required with iron screw posts, which are not very stiff unless driven in up to the bottom eye. Forward stays cannot be put on, without great loss of time, until the fence on the first row of posts has been completed; for they would interfere with the fence wires being looped over the posts.

Back stays should invariably be provided and anchored well back, so as to resist any attempt to pull the entanglement away by grapnels.

Side stays at the ends of separate lengths of entanglement are usually desirable.

Pickets used as holdfasts for stays should be "staggered," *i.e.*, not driven in vertically, but inclined away from the post that they stay.

(xi.) When stringing horizontal wires for an apron on a stay or diagonal, the latter should be given a kink or bend at the places of crossing, so that there will be less chance of the wires slipping down. The horizontal wires may be secured by binding wire, or by taking a bight and looping it round the stay. The coil should not be passed over and under, as this is a slow process.

Notes with reference to iron screw posts and pickets.

(*a*) The posts are 5 feet long with four eyes, the pickets are 3 feet 6 inches long with two eyes, or 15 inches long with a loop at the end. If the ground is soft, the posts can be screwed in two feet deep or more.*

---

* Angle iron posts are 5 feet 10 inches and 3 feet 6 inches long.

(b) In rapid work the wire can simply be placed in the eye by forming a loop in the wire and slipping it over the post. It is not intended that the wire should be threaded through the eye. If time allows, the horizontal wires can be put on slack, and when the fence is strung the post can be given a complete turn, so as to prevent the wire slipping out should it be cut; or the barbed wire may be twisted round the posts, through an eye, as it is put on; or it may be secured to the eyes by binding wire.

(c) To permit of the loops being slipped over the posts, it is obvious that the lowest wire in a fence must be put on first, and no forward or back stays can be fixed until the fence has been completed.

(d) Care must be taken that all the posts are originally screwed in so that the eyes point the same way, otherwise delays will occur in the wiring.

(e) Loose bundles of iron screw posts and pickets cannot be carried noiselessly. It is advisable, therefore, to wrap them round with a sandbag, secured by a light turn of wire with the ends twisted together. Enough end to this wire should be left so that it can be untwisted by hand without pliers.

(f) Short stakes or bats must be provided to fit the top eye of the posts in order to screw them in. The helves of the entrenching implement serve the purpose.

EXAMPLES OF WIRE DRILLS.

Picket is used to mean a short picket used as a holdfast.

Post is used to mean a longer upright.

Fence is used to mean a series of wires on a row of posts.

The conventional signs used in the diagrams are explained in Fig. 2.

In all the drills given, unless otherwise stated, it is assumed that:—

(a) The length to be erected is 50 yards;
(b) The stores required are collected at a point behind the centre of the length in a convenient order;
(c) The line of the fence has been marked or indicated;
(d) The drums of wire are opened and the ends ready;
(e) Bars or sticks are run through the drums, so that the wire can be uncoiled readily;
(f) Short sticks for screwing in the pickets are carried by the men requiring them (or mauls if wooden or angle iron pickets are used);
(g) All wirers have hedging gloves and wire cutters; and have their legs protected by gaiters or sandbags.

(h) Each number consists of two men who work together, and the numbers commence work in succession at a suitable interval (say 4 posts apart). Thus Nos. 2 move off as soon as Nos. 1 have the desired start, Nos. 3 at the same interval behind Nos. 2 ;
(i) All work is commenced on the left ;
(j) The men who put the top wire on a fence stay the end post to short pickets ;
(k) On completion of each operation or "duty" detailed in the drill, all men should return to a fixed place, in order to prevent confusion, if some work faster than others.
(l) Spare men are at hand to replace any casualties.

The drills are primarily intended for use with iron screw posts, but can be used for wooden or angle iron posts with slight modifications. If the soil permits of posts being screwed in to the bottom eye, no stays are necessary, and three horizontal wires in the fence, instead of four, will be sufficient.

No estimates of stores required are given, as the distance apart of the posts and the amount of wire used must depend on what is available.

DRILL No. 1.—DOUBLE APRON ENTANGLEMENT.

(*See Figure* 3.)

Working Party: 12 men exclusive of N.C.Os.

First Duty.

Nos. 1. Lay posts in position on ground A.
" 2. { Front rank—assists Nos. 1.
       { Rear rank—holds up posts for Nos. 3 to screw in.
" 3. Screw in posts, separately.
" 4. Lay front and rear pickets in position.
" 5. Screw in front pickets B.
" 6. Screw in rear pickets C.

Second Duty.

Nos. 1. Bottom wire of fence A.
" 2. Second "   "   "
" 3. Third   "   "   "
" 4. Top   "   "   "
" 5. Front diagonal between A and B.
" 6. Rear   "   "   A and C.

Third Duty.

Nos. 1. Top horizontal wire on front diagonals A B.
" 2. Second "   "   "   "   "
" 3. Bottom "   "   "   "   "
" 4. Top horizontal wire on back diagonal A C.
" 5. Second "   "   "   "   "
" 6. Bottom "   "   "   "   "

This drill involves Nos. 5 in "Second Duty," and Nos. 1, 2 and 3 in "Third Duty," working in front of the fence.

In the "First Duty" No. 2 rear rank holds up a post for No. 3 front rank to screw in until it gets a bite in the ground. He then holds up a post for No. 3 rear rank, etc.

This obstacle and others of the same nature can be deepened by adding similar bays behind it. The posts in successive bays should cover the intervals between those in front of them. (*See* Fig. 4.)

If two bays are made, the obstacle can be increased by tossing loose wire into the valley between the posts.

DRILL No. 2.—TRIP, FENCE AND APRON.

(*See Figure 5.*)

Working Party: 10 men exclusive of N.C.Os.

First Duty.

Nos. 1. Lay posts in position A.
 „ 2. Hold up posts.
 „ 3. Screw in posts.
 „ 4. Bring up and screw in front pickets B.
 „ 5. „   „   „   „   „ rear „ C.

Second Duty.

Nos. 1. Front trip wire on pickets B.
 „ 2. Bottom wire on fence A.
 „ 3. Second „   „   „
 „ 4. Third „   „   „
 „ 5. Top „   „   „

Third Duty.

Nos. 1. Front diagonal between A and B.
 „ 2. Back „   „ A and C.
 „ 3. Top horizontal wire on the diagonals A C.
 „ 4. Second „   „   „   „
 „ 5. Bottom „   „   „   „

Nos. 1 have to work in front of the fence in "Third Duty."

DRILL No. 3.—TRIP AND FENCE.

(*See Figure 6.*)

Working Party: 16 men exclusive of N.C.Os.

First Duty.

Nos. 1. Screw in posts 6 feet apart, A.
 „ 2. Screw in pickets B and C; B first.
 „ 3. Trip wire B.
 „ 4. Bottom wire of fence A.
 „ 5. Second wire „   „   „
 „ 6. Third wire „   „   „
 „ 7. Top wire „   „   „
 „ 8. Diagonal wire between A and C.

Second Duty.

Nos. 1. Diagonal wire between A and B.
" 2. Trip wire C.
" 3. Uncoil loose wire.
" 4. Uncoil loose wire.
" 5. Toss in loose wire uncoiled.
" 6. Toss in loose wire uncoiled.
" 7. Fasten loose wire.
" 8. Fasten loose wire.

In the "Second duty," Nos. 1 have to work in front of the fence.

Nos. 3 and 4 uncoil the loose barbed wire on the ground well clear of the entanglement. Six coils for each 25 yards.

Nos. 5 and 6 with large wooden pickets lift the loose wire and toss it on to the entanglement.

Nos. 7 and 8 spread the loose wire out and fasten it by twisting a bight at intervals to the diagonals and fence wires.

DRILL No. 4.—FENCE, WITH CROSSED DIAGONALS AND TRIPS.

(*See Figure* 7.)

Working Party: 14 men exclusive of N.C.Os.

The pickets are placed opposite the posts.

This drill involves four men working on the enemy's side of the fence.

First Duty.

Nos. 1. Screw in posts A.
" 2. Screw in pickets, B first, then C.
" 3. Trip wire B.
" 4. Bottom wire of fence A.
" 5. Second wire " "
" 6. Third wire " "
" 7. Top wire " "

Second Duty.

Nos. 1. } Prepare posts in next length.
" 2. }
" 3. Front diagonal between A and B, commencing at picket B, B_1, then to A_2, B_3, etc.
" 4. Front diagonal between A and B, commencing at top of post A_1, then to B_2, A_3.
" 5. Back diagonal between A and C, commencing at picket C_1, then to A_2, C_3, A_4, etc.
" 6. } Back diagonal between A and C, commencing at
" 7. } top of post A_1, then to C_2, A_3, etc.

DRILL No. 5.—SUCCESSIVE ROWS OF FENCES.

(*See Figure* 8.)

Working Party: 12 men, divided into four groups of 3 each, W, X, Y, Z.

The posts must be prepared by attaching binding wire to the bottom eye, to this the vertical diagonals between the fences are made fast.

First Duty.

Group W. Lay out posts in row B.
" X. Screw in above.
" Y. Lay out pickets in row A.
" Z. Screw in above.

Second Duty.

Group W. Lay out posts in row C.
" X. Screw in above.
" Y. Bottom wire of fence B.
" Z. Trip wire on row A.

Third Duty.

Group W. Second wire on fence B.
" X. Third wire on fence B.
" Y. Top wire on fence B.
" Z. Front diagonal between A and B.

Fourth Duty.

Group W. Bottom wire of fence C.
" X. Second wire of fence C.
" Y. Third wire of fence C.
" Z. Top wire of fence C.

Fifth Duty.

Group W. Diagonal between B and C, bottom of C_1 to top of B_1, bottom of C_2, etc.
" X. Second diagonal between B and C, top of C_1 to bottom of B_1, top of C_2, etc.
" Y. Lay out and screw in pickets D.
" Z. Diagonal between C and D.

or { lay out row of posts D, if the fences are to be continued. screw in above, etc.

In "Third Duty," Z, and in "Fifth Duty," W and X, work on enemy's side of fence.

In "Fifth Duty," W and X loop the diagonals over top of pickets and make them fast to the bottom eye by binding wire.

Instead of putting the criss-cross diagonals between fences B and C as above, which involves binding wire and takes some little time, it would be sufficient if time presses to stay the pickets merely by connecting the heads. (See Fig. 9.) "Gooseberries," etc., can be thrown into the space between B and C.

Another variation is to put loose wire or French wire between fences B and C and criss-cross plain wire to connect the tops of the pickets. (See Fig. 10.)

A further variation can be introduced by placing the posts so as to form squares instead of triangles. (See Fig. 11.)

DRILL No. 6.—DOUBLE FENCE.

(*See Figure* 12.)

Working Party: 28 men exclusive of N.C.Os.

This entanglement is designed for stout wooden posts well driven in, or screw posts screwed in down to the bottom eye ; no holdfast pickets are then required.

The drill only requires one duty from each pair of men.

The apron is of a different pattern to those previously given, the wires miss alternate pickets.

Three horizontal wires can be used for the fence instead of the "gate" pattern shown.

Order of Work.

(1) Under superintendence of two N.C.Os. all hands carry up and place the posts on the ground.

(2) Nos. 1 drive or screw in posts in front fence A.
,,   2   ,,   ,,   ,,   ,,   back   ,,   B.
,,   3 bottom wire 3 of fence A.
,,   4 diagonal ,, 4 ,,   ,,   ,,
,,   5 diagonal ,, 5 ,,   ,,   ,,
,,   6 top   ,,   6 ,,   ,,   ,,
,,   7 bottom ,,   3 of fence B.
,,   8 diagonal ,, 4 ,,   ,,   ,,
,,   9 diagonal ,, 5 ,,   ,,   ,,
,, 10 top   ,,   6 ,,   ,,   ,,
,, 11 apron wire 11
,, 12   ,,   ,,   12
,, 13   ,,   ,,   13
,, 14 festooned wire 14

DRILL No. 7.—ORDINARY LOW ENTANGLEMENT.*

(*See Figure* 13.)

Working party: 30 men in 10 groups, with a N.C.O.

Group A, front row of pickets A.
,,   B, straight wire A row of pickets.
,,   C, second row of pickets C.
,,   D, zig-zag wire A_1, C_1, A_2, C_2, etc.
,,   E, loose wire on zig-zag A_1, C_1, A_2, C_2, etc.
,,   F, straight wire on C row of pickets.
,,   G, third row of pickets G.
,,   H, zig-zag wire G_1, C_1, G_2, C_2, etc.
,,   J, loose wire on zig-zag G_1, C_1, G_2, C_2, etc.
,,   K, straight wire on G row of pickets.

Pickets may be 12" to 18" out of the ground and three feet apart.

---

* A Low Entanglement is not, as a rule, sufficient by itself but may be combined with a high Entanglement (*see* Figs. 15, 16, 17, 18).

DRILL No. 8.—FRENCH WIRE OBSTACLE.

(See Figure 14.)

The obstacle consists of two rows of French wire, placed just far enough apart for a man to pass between them. Each coil is stapled down in five places—at each end, and at $\frac{1}{4}$, $\frac{1}{2}$ and $\frac{3}{4}$ of its length. When two coils meet, the same staple fastens down both coils.

Posts, five feet long, are driven through the centre of the coils in five places, as in the case of the staples; the ends of adjoining coils are interlaced a little so that the post will go through both.

A strand of barbed wire is run along the top of each row and fastened to the posts with a round turn. It is pulled as taut as possible and twisted on to the French wire, by a staple, peg or wire cutters, close to each post, and in several places between the posts.

One or more strands of barbed wire are run along to the front as an "apron."

Diagonal wires are run from the tops of posts of the front row to tops of posts of second row.

Working party: 24 men in three parties, with N.C.O.

Front Row.

Party A. 1 holds end of French wire and staples it down.
    2 pulls wire out 20 yards.
    3 shakes wire clear of obstructions and puts in staples $\frac{1}{4}$, $\frac{1}{2}$ and $\frac{3}{4}$ way along.

Party B. 1 mauls in anchorage pickets and posts.
    2 holds posts.
    3 supplies posts.

„ C. 1 uncoils barbed wire.
   2 makes fast end to anchorage and twists wire round tops of pickets.
   3 twists barbed wire on to the French wire.

„ D. 1 runs coil of barbed wire along the front.
   2 ⎱
   3 ⎰ twist it on to the front of the French wire.

Back Row.

„ E. Same as A.
„ F. Same as B.
„ G. Same as C.
„ H. 1, with coil of barbed wire, moves between the two rows, uncoiling the wire.
   2 ⎧ move on either side of the entanglement and
   3 ⎨ make this barbed wire fast to the posts as the
    ⎩ diagonal, while H_1 holds the coil so that H_2 and H_3 can reach it.

The obstacles described above can be combined in various ways either by placing one behind the others *(see* Figs. 15 and 16), or by placing a high wire entanglement over a low one *(see* Figs. 17 and 18).

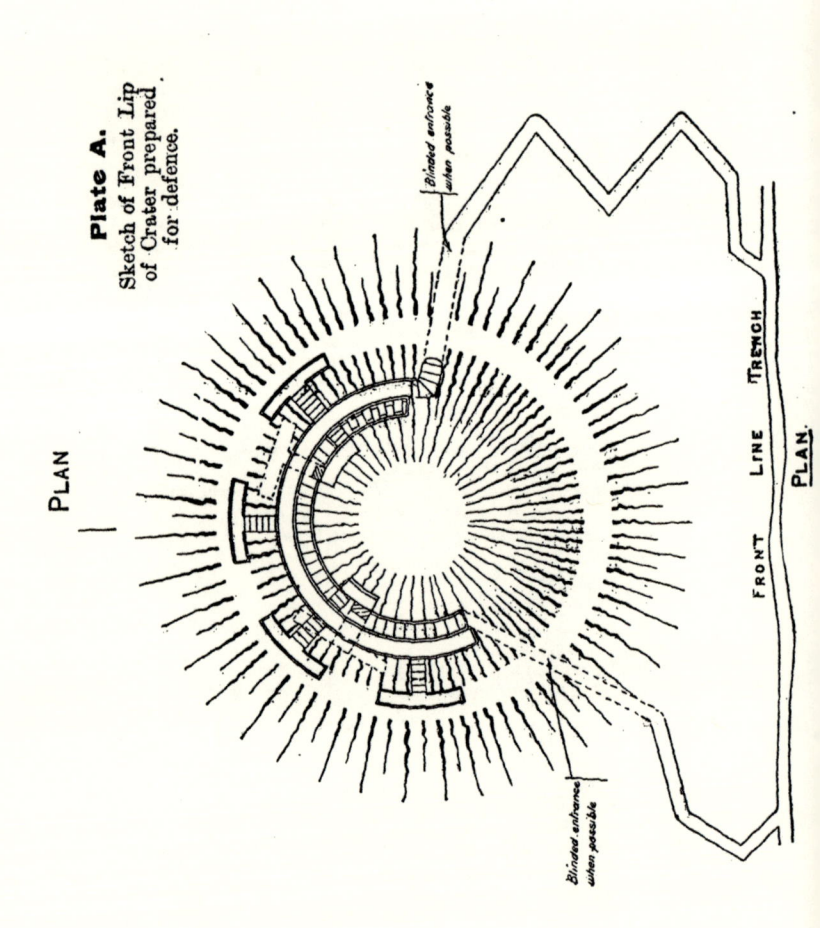

Plate A.
Sketch of Front Lip of Crater prepared for defence.

PLAN

Blinded entrance when possible

Blinded entrance when possible

FRONT LINE TRENCH

PLAN.

ELEVATION

Approx. Scale 1″ = 12′.

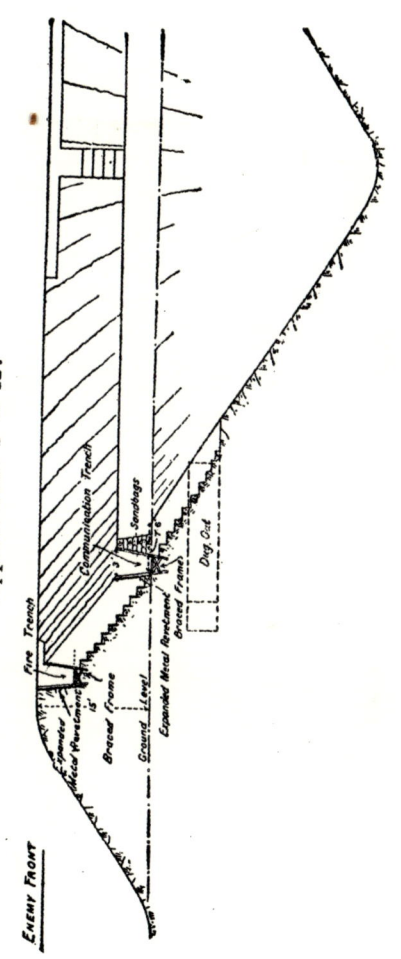

PLAN

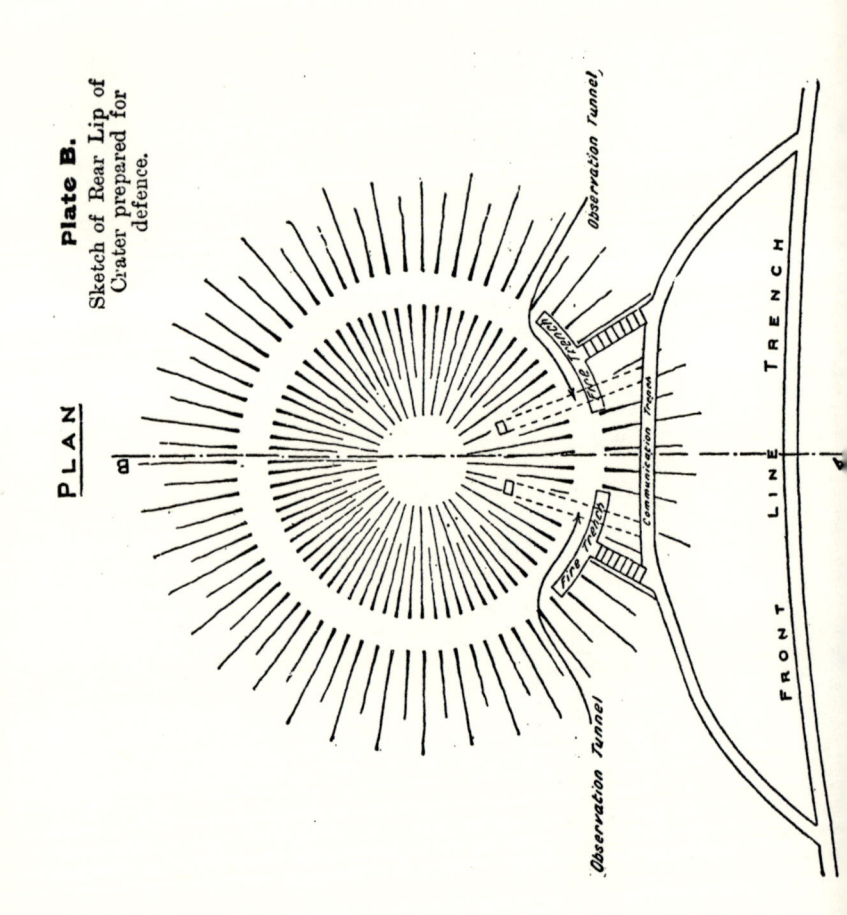

Plate B.
Sketch of Rear Lip of Crater prepared for defence.

21

SECTIONAL ELEVATION ON A.B.
Approx. Scale 1" = 24'.

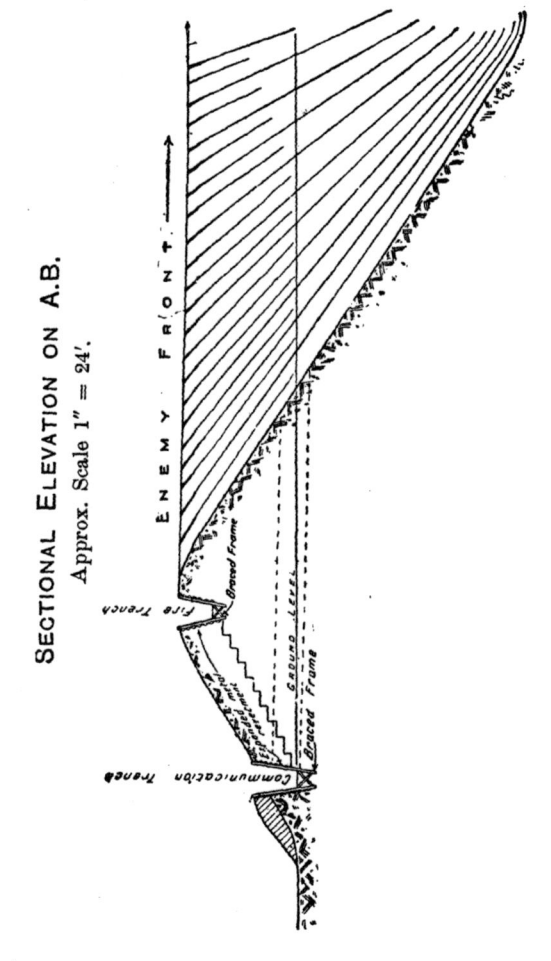

Plate C.

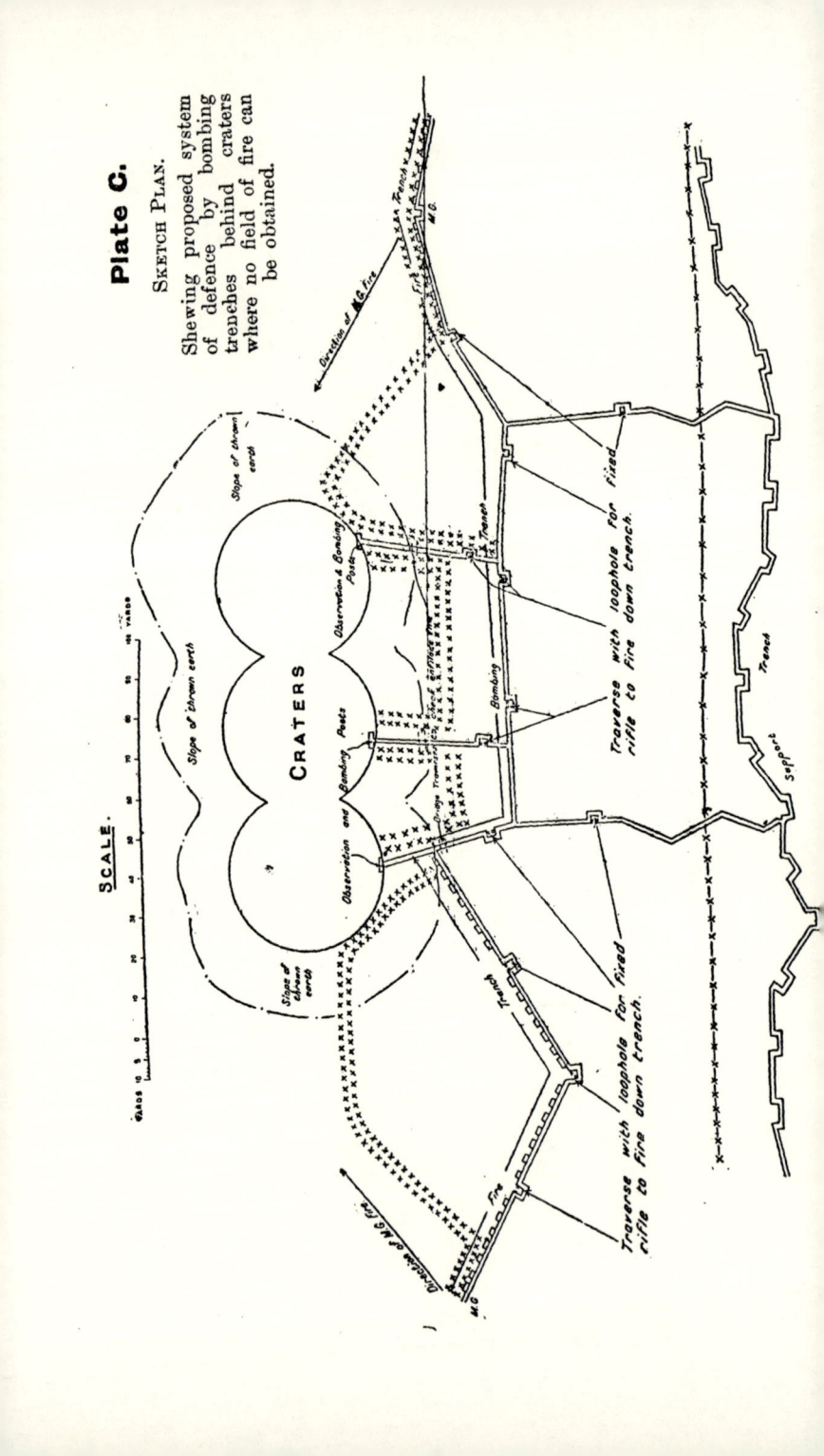

SKETCH PLAN.

Shewing proposed system of defence by bombing trenches behind craters where no field of fire can be obtained.

Fig. 1.

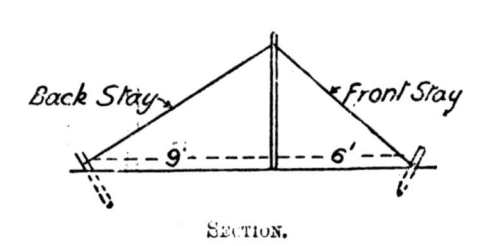

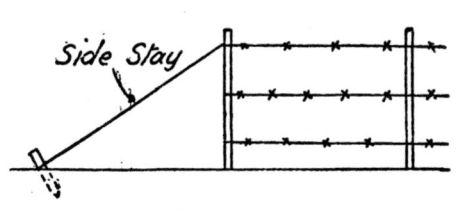

SECTION.

ELEVATION.

Fig. 2.

CONVENTIONAL SIGNS USED IN PLATES.

	PLAN.	ELEVATION.
Posts (long).	○	
Pickets (short).	•	
In fence. 1 Horizontal Wire.		
2 Horizontal Wires.		
4 Horizontal Wires.		
Inclined Wire.	Top end. — Low end.	
Gate.		
Gate and 2 Horizontal Wires.		

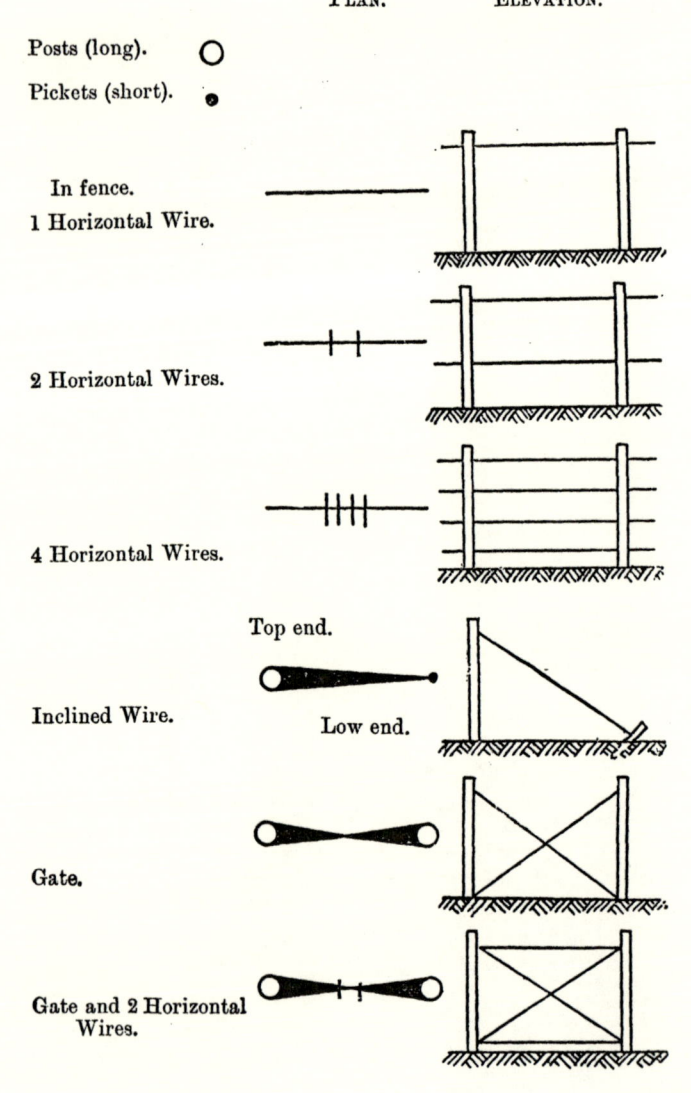

Fig. 3.

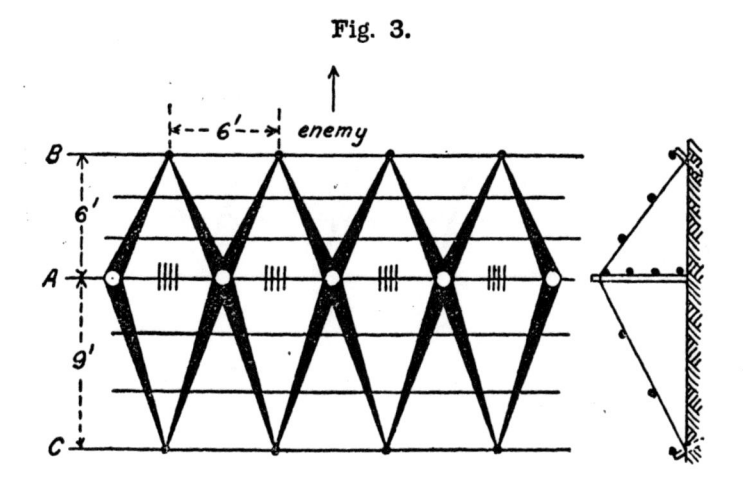

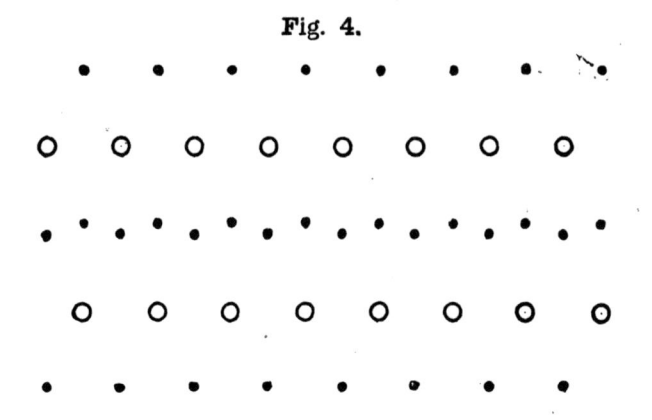

Fig. 4.

26

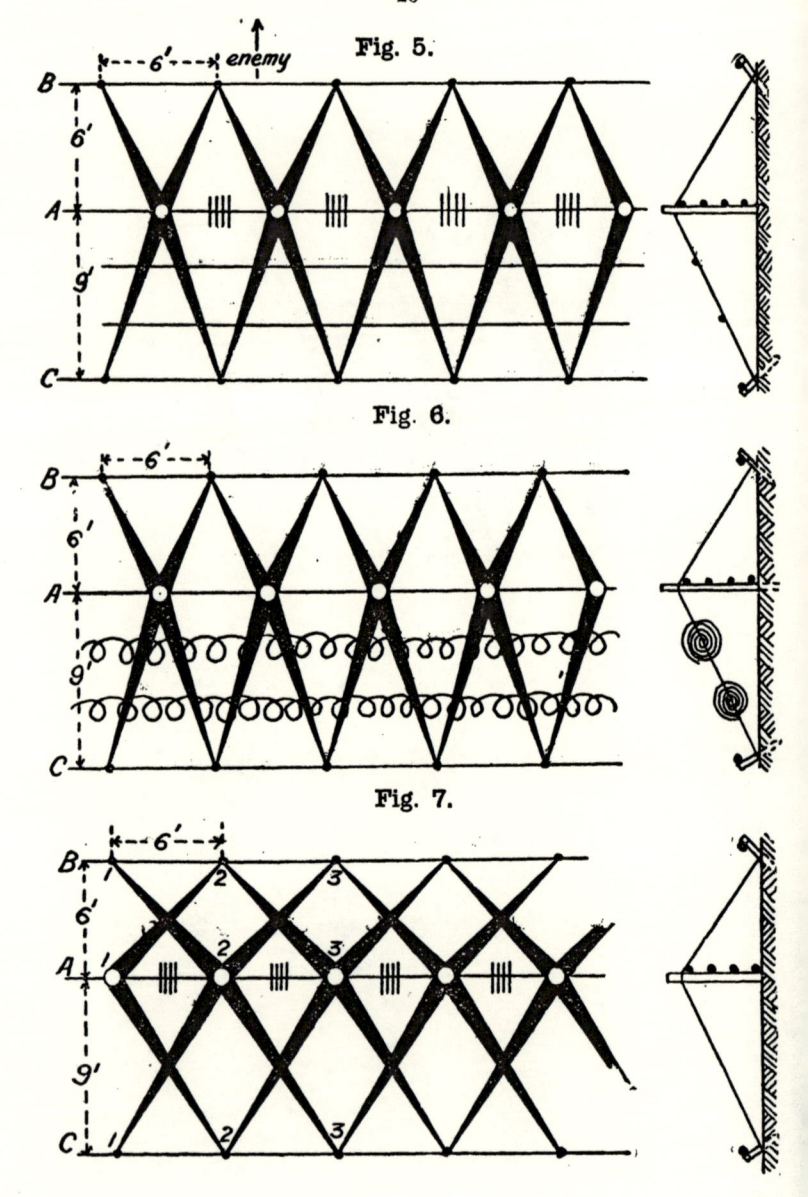

Fig. 5.

Fig. 6.

Fig. 7.

27

Fig. 8.

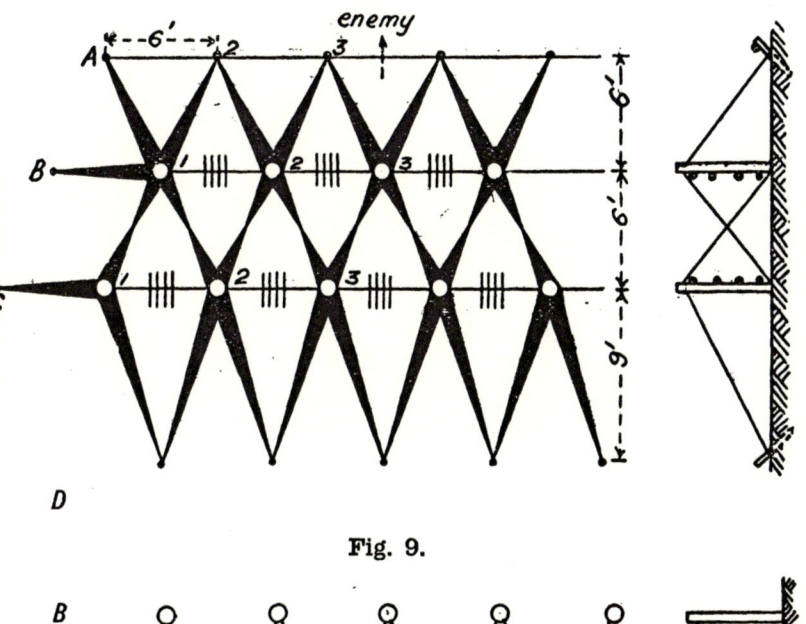

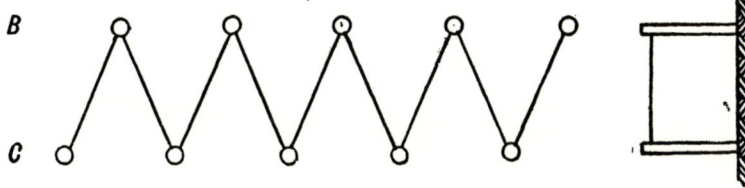

Fig. 9.

Fig. 10.

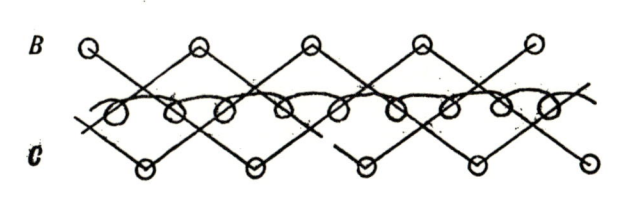

Fig. 11.

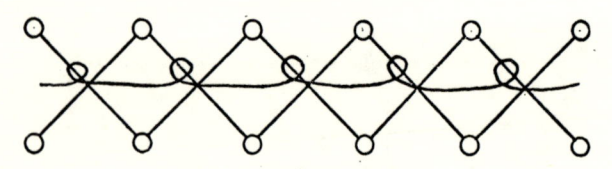

Fig. 12.

ELEVATION OF A AND B.

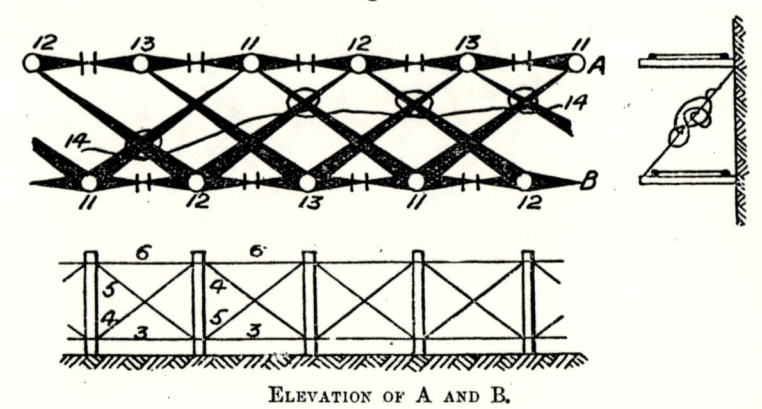

Fig. 13.

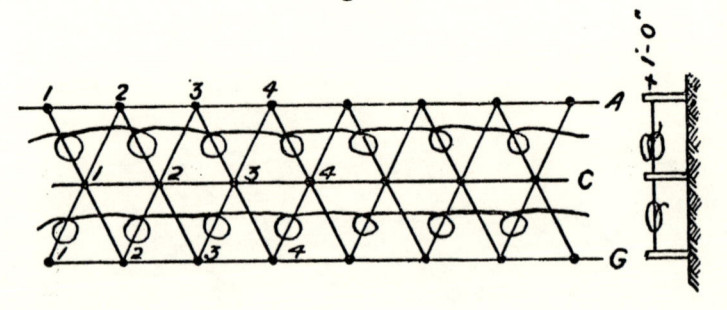

Fig. 14.

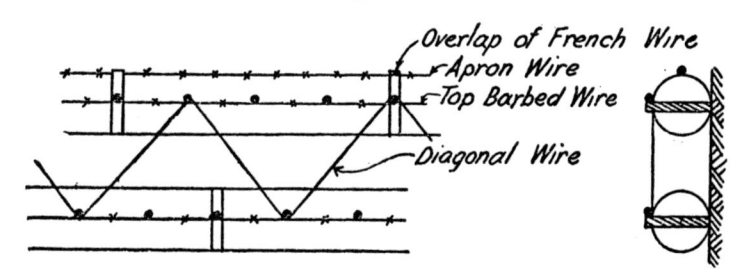

Overlap of French Wire
Apron Wire
Top Barbed Wire
Diagonal Wire

Fig. 15.

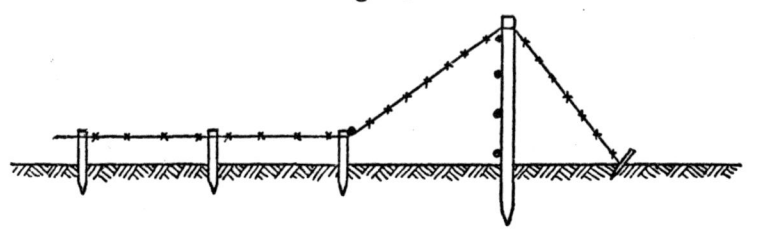

Fig. 16.

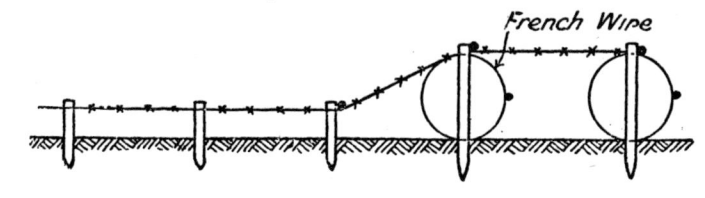

French Wire

Combined High & Low Entanglements.

Fig. 17.

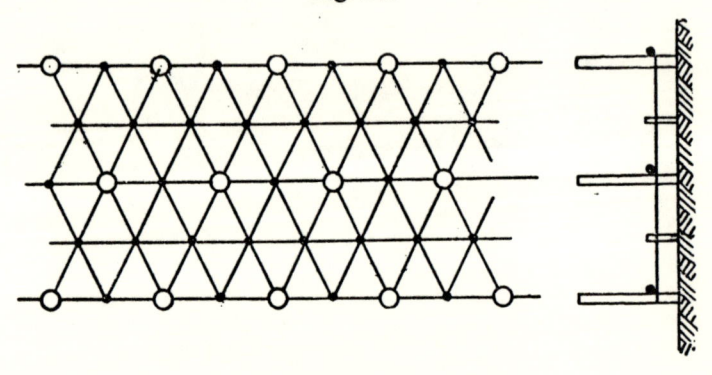

Fig. 18

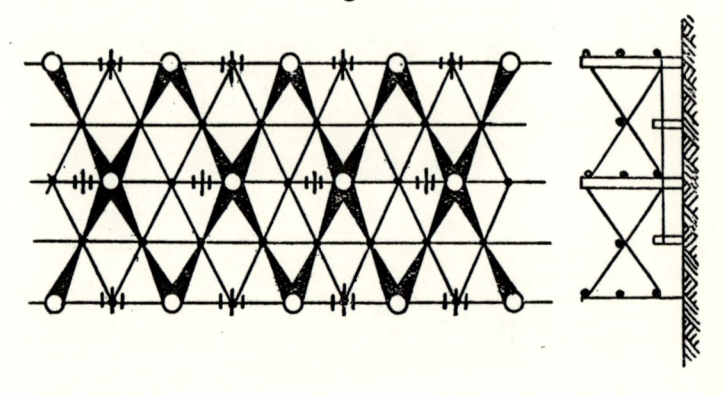

Printed in the United Kingdom by
Lightning Source UK Ltd., Milton Keynes
141348UK00001B/19/A